EASY BUFFALO COOKBOOK

ADD A DELICIOUSLY SPICY KICK TO YOUR COOKING

By
Chef Maggie Chow
Copyright © 2015 by Saxonberg Associates

Published by
BookSumo, a division of Saxonberg Associates
http://www.booksumo.com/

STAY TO THE END OF THE COOKBOOK AND RECEIVE....

I really appreciate when people, take the time to read all of my recipes.

So, as a gift for reading this entire cookbook you will receive a **massive collection of special recipes.**

Read to the end of and get my *Easy Specialty Cookbook Box Set for FREE*!

This box set includes the following:

1. ***Easy Sushi Cookbook***
2. ***Easy Dump Dinner Cookbook***
3. ***Easy Beans Cookbook***

Remember this box set is about **EASY** cooking.

In the ***Easy Sushi Cookbook*** you will learn the easiest methods to prepare almost every type of Japanese Sushi i.e. *California Rolls, the Perfect Sushi Rice, Crab Rolls, Osaka Style Sushi*, and so many others.

Then we go on to *Dump Dinners.* Nothing can be easier than a Dump Dinner. In the ***Easy Dump Dinner Cookbook*** we will learn how to master our slow cookers and make some amazingly unique dinners that will take almost *no effort*.

Finally in the ***Easy Beans Cookbook*** we tackle one of my favorite side dishes: Beans. There are so many delicious ways to make Baked Beans and Bean Salads that I had to share them.

So stay till the end and then keep on cooking with my *Easy Specialty Cookbook Box Set*!

ABOUT THE AUTHOR.

Maggie Chow is the author and creator of your favorite *Easy Cookbooks* and *The Effortless Chef Series*. Maggie is a lover of all things related to food. Maggie loves nothing more than finding new recipes, trying them out, and then making them her own, by adding or removing ingredients, tweaking cooking times, and anything to make the recipe not only taste better, but be easier to cook!

For a complete listing of all my books please see my author page.

INTRODUCTION

Welcome to *The Effortless Chef Series*! Thank you for taking the time to download the *Easy Buffalo Cookbook*. Come take a journey with me into the delights of easy cooking. The point of this cookbook and all my cookbooks is to exemplify the effortless nature of cooking simply.

In this book we focus on Buffalo style cooking. You will find that even though the recipes are simple, the taste of the dishes is quite amazing.

So will you join me in an adventure of simple cooking? If the answer is yes (and I hope it is) please consult the table of contents to find the dishes you are most interested in. Once you are ready jump right in and start cooking.

— Chef Maggie Chow

TABLE OF CONTENTS

ANY ISSUES? CONTACT ME

If you find that something important to you is missing from this book please contact me at maggie@booksumo.com.

I will try my best to re-publish a revised copy taking your feedback into consideration and let you know when the book has been revised with you in mind.

:)

— Chef Maggie Chow

LEGAL NOTES

COMMON ABBREVIATIONS

cup(s)	C.
tablespoon	tbsp
teaspoon	tsp
ounce	oz.
pound	lb

*All units used are standard American measurements

CHAPTER 1: EASY BUFFALO RECIPES

BUFFALO POTATOES AND CHICKEN FINGERS

Ingredients

- 4 baking potatoes, scrubbed
- 3 tbsps extra virgin olive oil
- salt & freshly ground black pepper
- 1/4-1/2 C. milk
- 1/2 C. blue cheese, crumbles
- 5 scallions, chopped
- salt & freshly ground black pepper
- 2 lbs chicken tenders, cut into bite-size pieces
- 3 large garlic cloves, chopped
- 1/4-1/2 C. hot sauce
- 4 tbsps butter

- carrot sticks
- celery rib
- sour cream, garnish

Directions

- Set your oven to 400 degrees before doing anything else.
- Layer your potatoes into a casserole dish and top them with some olive oil and perforate each one with a fork.
- Now top everything with some salt and cook the potatoes in the oven for 45 mins.
- Now slice the potatoes in half and once they have cooled a bit remove the insides but try to keep the shape of the potato intact.
- Combine the insides slowly with milk and mash everything together. Add in some pepper, salt, the scallions and the blue cheese. Combine the mix evenly.
- Fill your potato shells with the mashed potatoes then place the filled potato skins into the oven for 7 mins.

- At the same time begin to fry your chicken after coating the pieces with pepper and salt, in 3 tbsps of oil, with the garlic as well.
- Let the chicken cook for 7 mins while stirring.
- Shut the heat combine the chicken with the butter and hot sauce. Stir everything to evenly coat the meat.
- Serve your potatoes with some of the chicken and top each serving with some sour cream.
- Place your celery and carrots on the side as well for a garnish.
- Enjoy.

Amount per serving: 4

Timing Information:

Preparation	15 mins
Total Time	1 hr 5 mins

Nutritional Information:

Calories	649.3
Cholesterol	190.6mg
Sodium	989.3mg
Carbohydrates	31.0g
Protein	55.5g

* Percent Daily Values are based on a 2,000 calorie diet.

Buffalo Dumplings

Ingredients

- 1/2 C. butter
- 1/2 C. hot pepper sauce
- 2 tsps distilled white vinegar
- 2 C. shredded cooked chicken
- 1 (8 oz.) package cream cheese, softened
- 1 (12 oz.) package wonton wrappers
- 1 egg white
- 2 C. oil for frying

Directions

- Get your butter melted, then add in the vinegar and hot sauce.
- Stir the mix then shut the heat.

- Leave the sauce to sit for 60 mins then add the chicken to the sauce and stir the contents to evenly coat the meat.
- Leave the chicken to sit for 17 more mins.
- Place your wrappers on a working surface then add half a tsp of chicken to each one. Place 1/2 a tsp of cream cheese to each one as well.
- Coat the edge of the each wonton with some of the egg whites and shape the wrapper into a wonton or dumpling.
- Crimp the opening to seal everything and keep forming wontons in this manner.
- Get your oil hot then fry your wontons in the oil, in batches, for about 3 mins. Flip them once during the frying time.
- Enjoy.

Amount per serving (16 total)

Timing Information:

Preparation	20 m
Cooking	15 m
Total Time	1 h 50 m

Nutritional Information:

Calories	219 kcal
Fat	15 g
Carbohydrates	12.7g
Protein	8.2 g
Cholesterol	46 mg
Sodium	402 mg

* Percent Daily Values are based on a 2,000 calorie diet.

Buffalo Scallops

Ingredients

- 1 (16 oz.) package farfalle pasta
- 24 scallops, rinsed and drained
- 3/4 C. olive oil
- 1/4 C. lemon juice
- 1 1/2 tsps dried diced garlic
- 1 tsp salt
- 1/2 tsp ground black pepper
- 2 tbsps dried basil
- 9 tbsps whipped butter
- 2 tbsps sriracha

Directions

- Get your pasta boiling in water and salt for 9 mins then remove all the liquids.

- Get a bowl for your scallops.
- Get a 2nd bowl, combine: black pepper, 1/4 C. olive oil, half tsp salt, lemon juice, 1 tsp garlic.
- Combine both bowls and stir the mix to evenly coat the scallops.
- Lay out your scallops on a working surface and top them with 1 tbsp of basil.
- Get 1 tbsp of butter melted in a pan then begin to fry your scallops with the basil side facing downwards in the butter for 5 mins.
- Flip the scallops and continue frying them for 3 more mins. Fry half of the scallops at a time.
- Get the rest of the butter melted then add in 1/2 tsp salt, 1/2 C. olive oil, 1/2 tsp garlic, and 1 tbsps of basil.
- Stir the mix then add the pasta to the butter sauce.
- Toss the noodles to coat them with the sauce.
- Place some pasta on a serving dish and liberally add some scallops over the noodles and some sriracha.
- Enjoy.

Amount per serving (8 total)

Timing Information:

Preparation	15 m
Cooking	20 m
Total Time	35 m

Nutritional Information:

Calories	522 kcal
Fat	30.5 g
Carbohydrates	45.8g
Protein	16.1 g
Cholesterol	38 mg
Sodium	453 mg

* Percent Daily Values are based on a 2,000 calorie diet.

Buffalo Jumbo Shells

Ingredients

- 1 lb ground chicken
- 1/4 C. butter
- 1 C. hot pepper sauce
- 1 (16 oz.) container whipped ricotta cheese
- cooking spray
- 1 (16 oz.) package jumbo pasta shells
- 1 (8 oz.) package shredded Cheddar-Monterey Jack cheese blend
- salt and ground black pepper to taste

Directions

- Stir fry your chicken for 8 mins then remove any excess oils from the pan.

- Add your butter to the chicken, let it melt then add in the hot sauce.
- Shut the heat and stir everything.
- Now drain your ricotta and place it in a bowl.
- Add the buffalo chicken to the cheese and stir everything.
- Place a covering of plastic on the bowl and put everything into the fridge for 5 hrs.
- Coat a casserole dish with nonstick spray then set your oven to 375 degrees before doing anything else.
- Get your pasta boiling in water and salt for 12 mins then remove all the liquids.
- Once the shells have cooled off a bit stuff them with the chicken and place the shells into the dish.
- Top everything with the Monterey, some pepper and salt as well.
- Cook the pasta in the oven for 17 mins.
- Enjoy.

Amount per serving (6 total)

Timing Information:

Preparation	15 m
Cooking	25 m
Total Time	3 h 40 m

Nutritional Information:

Calories	698 kcal
Fat	29 g
Carbohydrates	62.8g
Protein	44.4 g
Cholesterol	126 mg
Sodium	1491 mg

* Percent Daily Values are based on a 2,000 calorie diet.

Buffalo Prawns

Ingredients

- 2 C. all-purpose flour
- 2 tbsps Creole-style seasoning
- 1 tbsp garlic powder
- 1 tbsp ground cayenne pepper
- 1 tsp onion powder
- 1 tsp freshly ground black pepper
- 1 lb large shrimp, peeled and deveined with tails attached
- 4 C. oil for frying

Sauce:

- 4 cloves garlic, diced
- 2 1/2 tbsps butter
- 6 oz. hot pepper sauce
- 1 tsp ground cayenne pepper

Directions

- Get a bowl, combine: black pepper, flour, onion powder, creole seasoning, cayenne, and garlic powder.
- Stir the mix then add in your shrimp and evenly coat the pieces of shrimp with the dry mix.
- Now lay your shrimp in a casserole dish and cover the dish with some plastic wrap. Place the shrimp in the fridge for 30 mins.
- Get a bowl, combine: cayenne, garlic, hot sauce, and butter.
- Stir the mix until it is smooth then get your oil hot for frying.
- Place your shrimp again in the dry mix then fry them.
- Once all the shrimp has been cooked. Place them into the butter hot sauce mix and coat them evenly.
- Enjoy.

Amount per serving (4 total)

Timing Information:

Preparation	15 m
Cooking	20 m
Total Time	45 m

Nutritional Information:

Calories	626 kcal
Fat	32.1 g
Carbohydrates	54.4g
Protein	30.1 g
Cholesterol	198 mg
Sodium	2129 mg

* Percent Daily Values are based on a 2,000 calorie diet.

BUFFALO CHICKEN BITES

Ingredients

- 2 tbsps olive oil
- 3/4 C. hot pepper sauce
- 1/2 C. butter
- 2 lbs ground chicken
- 1 2/3 C. dry bread crumbs
- 2 stalks celery, diced
- 2 large eggs
- 2 tbsps hot pepper sauce

Directions

- Coat a cookie sheet with olive oil then set your oven to 450 degrees before doing anything else.
- Get your butter melted in a pan then add in 3/4 C. of hot sauce. Stir the mix until it is smooth then shut the heat.

- Get a bowl, combine: eggs, chicken, celery, bread crumbs, and hot sauce mix.
- Stir the mix then begin to work it with your hands into balls.
- Place the balls on the sheet and cook them in the oven for 17 mins.
- Coat the balls with 2 tbsps of additional hot sauce.
- Enjoy.

Amount per serving (75 total)

Timing Information:

Preparation	15 m
Cooking	15 m
Total Time	35 m

Nutritional Information:

Calories	41 kcal
Fat	2.2 g
Carbohydrates	1.9g
Protein	< 3.2 g
Cholesterol	16 mg
Sodium	104 mg

* Percent Daily Values are based on a 2,000 calorie diet.

Buffalo Macaroni

Ingredients

- 1/2 lb cubed cooked chicken
- 2 tbsps hot sauce, or to taste
- 2 tbsps ranch dressing, or to taste
- 1 (7.25 oz.) package macaroni and cheese mix
- 1/4 C. margarine
- 1/4 C. 2% milk
- 2 stalks celery, chopped
- 2 tbsps crumbled blue cheese

Directions

- Set your oven to 350 degrees before doing anything else.
- Get a bowl, combine: ranch dressing, hot sauce, and chicken.

- Let the chicken sit while you get your pasta boiling in water and salt for 10 mins.
- Remove all the liquids from the pasta then add in the cheese powder, margarine and milk.
- Stir everything evenly.
- Add half of the noodles to a baking dish then add in the buffalo chicken, blue, and celery.
- Add the rest of the macaroni and cook everything in the oven for 20 mins.
- Enjoy.

Amount per serving (6 total)

Timing Information:

Preparation	15 m
Cooking	25 m
Total Time	40 m

Nutritional Information:

Calories	304 kcal
Fat	15.2 g
Carbohydrates	24.3g
Protein	17 g
Cholesterol	37 mg
Sodium	608 mg

* Percent Daily Values are based on a 2,000 calorie diet.

Buffalo Bake

Ingredients

- 1 (8 oz.) carton sour cream
- 1/4 tsp onion powder
- 1/4 tsp garlic powder
- 1/2 tsp dried dill weed
- 1/2 tsp dried parsley
- 1 (8 oz.) package cream cheese, softened
- 1 C. shredded Cheddar cheese
- 3 tbsps hot pepper sauce
- 1 (14.5 oz.) can chicken broth
- 1 C. uncooked white rice
- 2 C. cubed, cooked chicken

Directions

- Set your oven to 375 degrees before doing anything else.

- Get a bowl, combine: parsley, sour cream, dill, onion powder, and garlic powder.
- Stir the mix evenly then add in the hot sauce, cream cheese, and cheddar.
- Stir the mix again until it is smooth then add in the chicken broth gradually.
- Stir the mix again then add in the chicken and the rice. Then pour everything into a baking dish.
- Cook everything in the oven for 65 mins.
- Enjoy.

Amount per serving (4 total)

Timing Information:

Preparation	10 m
Cooking	1 h
Total Time	1 h 10 m

Nutritional Information:

Calories	756 kcal
Fat	49.9 g
Carbohydrates	41.8g
Protein	33.8 g
Cholesterol	171 mg
Sodium	698 mg

* Percent Daily Values are based on a 2,000 calorie diet.

Buffalo Wings I

Ingredients

- oil for deep frying
- 1 C. unbleached all-purpose flour
- 2 tsps salt
- 1/2 tsp ground black pepper
- 1/2 tsp cayenne pepper
- 1/4 tsp garlic powder
- 1/2 tsp paprika
- 1 egg
- 1 C. milk
- 3 skinless, boneless chicken breasts, cut into 1/2-inch strips
- 1/4 C. hot pepper sauce
- 1 tbsp butter

Directions

- Get your oil hot for frying.
- At the same time get a bowl, combine: paprika, flour, garlic powder, salt, cayenne, and black pepper.
- Get a 2nd bowl, combine: milk and eggs.
- Coat your chicken first with the gg mix then dredge them in the flour mix.
- Place the chicken back in the egg mix and again in the flour mix.
- Place everything in a bowl and place a covering of plastic on the bowl.
- Put the chicken in the fridge for 30 mins then begin to fry the chicken, in batches, for 8 mins.
- Once all the chicken is done get a 3rd bowl and combine your butter and hot sauce.
- Place the mix in the microwave for 1 min with a high level of heat then top the chicken with the mix.
- Enjoy.

Amount per serving (3 total)

Timing Information:

Preparation	10 m
Cooking	20 m
Total Time	50 m

Nutritional Information:

Calories	710 kcal
Fat	46.9 g
Carbohydrates	43.7g
Protein	28 g
Cholesterol	136 mg
Sodium	2334 mg

* Percent Daily Values are based on a 2,000 calorie diet.

BUFFALO CHICKEN SANDWICH

Ingredients

- 1 tbsp vegetable oil
- 1 tbsp butter
- 1 lb skinless, boneless chicken breasts, cut into bite-size pieces
- 1/4 C. hot sauce
- 4 (10 inch) flour tortillas
- 2 C. shredded lettuce
- 1 celery stalk, diced
- 1/2 C. blue cheese dressing

Directions

- Fry your chicken in veggie oil for 12 mins until it is fully done then place the meat to the side in a bowl.

- Add in the hot sauce to the bowl and stir everything to evenly coat the meat.
- Now place your tortillas on a working surface and place your chicken on each equally.
- Layer your dressing, celery, and lettuce over everything then form the contents into burritos.
- Enjoy.

Amount per serving (4 total)

Timing Information:

Preparation	20 m
Cooking	10 m
Total Time	30 m

Nutritional Information:

Calories	588 kcal
Fat	32.6 g
Carbohydrates	39.8g
Protein	30.4 g
Cholesterol	83 mg
Sodium	1208 mg

* Percent Daily Values are based on a 2,000 calorie diet.

Buffalo Pizza

Ingredients

- 3 skinless, boneless chicken breast halves, cooked and cubed
- 2 tbsps butter, melted
- 1 (2 oz.) bottle hot sauce
- 1 (8 oz.) bottle blue cheese salad dressing
- 1 (16 inch) prepared pizza crust
- 1 (8 oz.) package shredded mozzarella cheese

Directions

- Set your oven to 425 degrees before doing anything else.
- Get a bowl, combine: hot sauce, butter, and chicken. Stir the mix until the chicken is evenly coated.
- Now lay out your pizza crust on a cookie sheet and coat it evenly with the ranch dressing.

- Add the chicken over the dressing, then add the cheese.
- Cook everything into the oven for 12 mins.
- Enjoy.

Amount per serving (6 total)

Timing Information:

Preparation	30 m
Cooking	25 m
Total Time	55 m

Nutritional Information:

Calories	785 kcal
Fat	40.7 g
Carbohydrates	66.6g
Protein	37.1 g
Cholesterol	83 mg
Sodium	1840 mg

* Percent Daily Values are based on a 2,000 calorie diet.

BUFFALO SHROOMS

Ingredients

- 10 large mushrooms, stems and insides removed
- 1 tsp olive oil, or as needed
- 1 celery stalk, diced
- 1/4 C. blue cheese dressing
- 1/4 C. ranch dressing
- 1/4 C. buffalo wing sauce
- 2 oz. cream cheese
- 2 cooked chicken breasts, shredded
- 1/2 C. shredded Cheddar cheese

Directions

- Set your oven to 350 degrees before doing anything else.
- Get a casserole dish and lay your mushrooms in it with the insides facing upwards.

- Begin to stir fry your celery for 7 mins then combine in the cream cheese, dressings, and buffalo sauce.
- Stir the mix and keep heating it until the cheese is melted for 7 mins.
- Now place your chicken in a bowl with the sauce and stir everything until the chicken is evenly coated.
- Now fill your mushrooms with the mix and then top everything with the cheddar.
- Cook the mushrooms in the oven for 25 mins.
- Enjoy.

Amount per serving (10 total)

Timing Information:

Preparation	15 m
Cooking	30 m
Total Time	45 m

Nutritional Information:

Calories	165 kcal
Fat	13 g
Carbohydrates	2.9g
Protein	< 9 g
Cholesterol	32 mg
Sodium	356 mg

* Percent Daily Values are based on a 2,000 calorie diet.

BUFFALO SANDWICH II

(FRENCH ONIONS)

Ingredients

- 4 skinless, boneless chicken breast halves
- 1 (2 oz.) bottle hot pepper sauce
- 1 (5 oz.) bottle green hot pepper sauce
- 2 tsps paprika, divided
- 1 red onion, sliced in rings
- 4 slices tomato
- 4 leaves lettuce
- 4 thick slices French baguette, halved

Directions

- Get your oven's broiler hot then place your chicken in a pan for broiling.

- Top the chicken with paprika and both hot sauces.
- Layer your onions over everything. Then cook the chicken until it is fully done under the broiler for about 17 mins.
- Now layer your chicken on the bread and top everything with the lettuce and tomato.
- Enjoy.

Amount per serving (4 total)

Timing Information:

Preparation	5 m
Cooking	15 m
Total Time	20 m

Nutritional Information:

Calories	236 kcal
Fat	4.2 g
Carbohydrates	20.5g
Protein	27.8 g
Cholesterol	67 mg
Sodium	1561 mg

* Percent Daily Values are based on a 2,000 calorie diet.

Buffalo Fries

Ingredients

- cooking spray
- 4 large potatoes, sliced into wedges
- 2 tbsps olive oil, or to taste
- salt and ground black pepper to taste
- 1 C. Buffalo-style hot pepper sauce
- 1/4 C. melted butter, or to taste
- 1/4 C. ranch salad dressing, or to taste

Directions

- Coat a casserole dish with nonstick spray then set your oven to 400 degrees before doing anything else.
- Layer your potatoes into the dish and top them with some pepper, salt, and the olive oil.

- Cook the spuds in the oven for 35 mins then get a bowl and combine the melted butter and hot sauce.
- Stir the mix until it is smooth then add your potatoes to the mix.
- Stir everything to evenly coat the wedges then place the potatoes back into the dish.
- Top the potatoes with the ranch dressing.
- Enjoy.

Amount per serving (4 total)

Timing Information:

Preparation	10 m
Cooking	30 m
Total Time	40 m

Nutritional Information:

Calories	526 kcal
Fat	26.6 g
Carbohydrates	66.1g
Protein	8.1 g
Cholesterol	35 mg
Sodium	1765 mg

* Percent Daily Values are based on a 2,000 calorie diet.

Buffalo Fish

Ingredients

- 3 (4 oz.) flounder fillets
- 1/2 C. hot pepper sauce
- 1 C. corn flour
- 3 tbsps butter
- 3 tbsps extra-virgin olive oil
- 6 tbsps chunky blue cheese dressing

Directions

- Get a bowl and place your fish in it.
- Top the fish with the hot sauce and stir everything to evenly coat the pieces.
- Place a covering of plastic on the bowl and put everything in the fridge for 60 mins.

- Coat the fish with flour then place them in the hot sauce again, then coat them with flour, and again in the hot sauce.
- Get your olive oil and butter hot, in a frying pan, then fry the fish for 4 mins each side.
- Top the pieces with the blue cheese.
- Enjoy.

Amount per serving (3 total)

Timing Information:

Preparation	10 m
Cooking	6 m
Total Time	1 h 16 m

Nutritional Information:

Calories	641 kcal
Fat	43.1 g
Carbohydrates	37.7g
Protein	25.2 g
Cholesterol	95 mg
Sodium	1494 mg

* Percent Daily Values are based on a 2,000 calorie diet.

Buffalo Salad

Ingredients

- 2 C. cubed, cooked chicken
- 1/2 C. ranch dressing
- 1/4 C. hot buffalo wing sauce
- 3 stalks celery, diced
- 2 green onions, chopped
- salt and freshly ground black pepper to taste

Directions

- Get a bowl, mix: pepper, chicken, salt, ranch, green onions, celery, and buffalo sauce.
- Enjoy.

Amount per serving (4 total)

Timing Information:

Preparation	
Cooking	10 m
Total Time	10 m

Nutritional Information:

Calories	323 kcal
Fat	24.9 g
Carbohydrates	5.3g
Protein	18.5 g
Cholesterol	63 mg
Sodium	774 mg

* Percent Daily Values are based on a 2,000 calorie diet.

Buffalo Breakfast

Ingredients

- 2 frozen, breaded chicken strips
- 3 tbsps hot sauce
- 6 C. leftover mashed potatoes
- 3 eggs
- 1 (1 oz.) package ranch dressing mix
- 2 tbsps vegetable oil
- 1/2 C. shredded Cheddar cheese

Directions

- Fry your chicken until everything is fully done then slice the strips into small pieces.
- Get a bowl, combine: the hot sauce and chicken pieces. Stir the mix to evenly coat the meat.
- Get your oil hot then begin to fry 1/2 C. of the potatoes.

- As the potatoes fry press them down into patties. Top each one with some of the chicken pieces and cook everything for 5 mins each side.
- Top the patties with the cheese.
- Enjoy.

Amount per serving (12 total)

Timing Information:

Preparation	15 m
Cooking	15 m
Total Time	30 m

Nutritional Information:

Calories	207 kcal
Fat	8.9 g
Carbohydrates	25g
Protein	6.6 g
Cholesterol	59 mg
Sodium	713 mg

* Percent Daily Values are based on a 2,000 calorie diet.

BUFFALO CHICKEN I

Ingredients

- 8 small boneless skinless chicken thighs
- 1 1/2 tsps vegetable oil
- 1/4 C. hot sauce
- 3 tbsps margarine, melted
- 2 tbsps water
- 1 tbsp white vinegar
- 1/8 tsp pepper
- cooking spray
- blue cheese or ranch dressing, for dip

Directions

- Get a pan hot with oil after coating it with some nonstick spray.
- Set your oven to 400 degrees before doing anything else.

- Fry your chicken for 6 mins. Flip the chicken and fry it for 6 more mins.
- Place the meat into a casserole dish that has been sprayed with nonstick spray as well.
- Get a bowl, combine: hot sauce, margarine, vinegar, and pepper.
- Stir the mix until it is smooth then top your chicken with the mix.
- Cook the chicken in the oven for 30 mins then top the pieces with the blue cheese.
- Enjoy.

Amount per serving: 4

Timing Information:

Preparation	15 mins
Total Time	48 mins

Nutritional Information:

Calories	257.6
Cholesterol	114.5mg
Sodium	591.4mg
Carbohydrates	0.4g
Protein	27.2g

* Percent Daily Values are based on a 2,000 calorie diet.

Buffalo Ranch Potatoes

Ingredients

- 15 oz. frozen french fries
- 1/2 C. hot sauce
- 1/4 C. butter
- 1 tbsp white vinegar
- 3 oz. blue cheese
- 1/2 C. ranch dressing

Directions

- Cook your fries until they are fully done in the oven.
- Then begin to get the following hot while stirring: butter, hot sauce, and vinegar.
- Once the mix is smooth and even shut the heat.
- Coat your fries with the buffalo sauce when they have finished cooking and stir everything.

- Now top the potatoes with the blue cheese and let the cheese melt.
- If the fries have cooled too much place everything back in the oven for 3 mins to melt the cheese.
- Place the ranch on side for serving.
- Enjoy.

Amount per serving: 2

Timing Information:

Preparation	3 mins
Total Time	23 mins

Nutritional Information:

Calories	964.3
Cholesterol	112.7mg
Sodium	3649.7mg
Carbohydrates	58.8g
Protein	15.0g

* Percent Daily Values are based on a 2,000 calorie diet.

BUFFALO TOFU

Ingredients

- 1 lb extra firm tofu, drained and pressed
- 1 C. Frank's red hot sauce
- 1 1/2 C. whole wheat panko
- 1/4 C. flax seed
- 2 wasa, multigrain crackers
- 1 tbsp garlic powder
- 1 tbsp cayenne pepper
- salt, to taste

Directions

- Cut your tofu into cubes.
- Get a bowl, combine: hot sauce and tofu.
- Stir the mix then place a covering of plastic on the bowl.
- Put everything into the fridge for 2 hrs.

- Set your oven to 375 degrees before doing anything else.
- Now add the following to the bowl of a blender: flax seeds, panko, and crackers.
- Blend the mix until it is crumbly and smooth then add some cayenne, salt, and garlic powder.
- Coat your pieces of tofu with the crumbs then place them into a casserole dish.
- Cook the tofu in the oven for 22 mins then place the tofu on a serving plate with some carrots.
- Enjoy.

Amount per serving: 4

Timing Information:

Preparation	1 hr 1 hr
Total Time	20 mins

Nutritional Information:

Calories	152.9
Cholesterol	0.0mg
Sodium	1508.3mg
Carbohydrates	8.2g
Protein	12.0g

* Percent Daily Values are based on a 2,000 calorie diet.

BUFFALO EGGS

Ingredients

- 6 eggs
- 1/4 C. blue cheese, crumbled
- 2 tbsps mayonnaise
- 1 1/2 tsps parsley, diced
- 1/4 tsp Tabasco sauce
- 1/4 tsp salt
- 1/8 tsp pepper
- 1/4 tsp celery salt
- 1 celery rib, finely diced

Directions

- Place your eggs into a pan. Then submerge them in water.

- Get the water boiling, place a lid on the pot, and shut the heat.
- Let the eggs sit for 15 mins in the hot water.
- Now place your eggs into a bowl of cold water and remove the shells.
- Cut the eggs in half then remove the yolks to a bowl.
- Add the following to the yolks: blue cheese, mayo, parsley, tabasco, salt, pepper, and celery salt.
- Mash everything together until the mix is smooth. Then stuff your eggs with the mix.
- Top the eggs with the celery.
- Enjoy.

Amount per serving: 12

Timing Information:

Preparation	20 mins
Total Time	50 mins

Nutritional Information:

Calories	55.9
Cholesterol	95.7mg
Sodium	143.9mg
Carbohydrates	0.9g
Protein	3.8g

* Percent Daily Values are based on a 2,000 calorie diet.

Buffalo Spinach Sandwich

Ingredients

- cooking spray
- 1 (12 fluid oz.) bottle Buffalo wing sauce
- 1 (12 oz.) package extra-firm tofu, cut into cubes
- 4 slices Swiss cheese
- 4 honey-wheat tortillas
- 5 Campari tomatoes, sliced
- 1 C. fresh spinach, or to taste

Directions

- Coat a casserole dish with nonstick spray then set your oven to 400 degrees before doing anything else.
- Get a bowl, combine: tofu and buffalo sauce.
- Let the mix sit as the oven heats.

- Layer your tofu into the casserole dish and pour the sauce over them.
- Cook the tofu for 12 mins then turn the cubes and cook them for 12 more mins.
- Lay out your tortillas and top each with 1 piece of cheese. Place the tortillas in the microwave for 1 min or until the cheese melts.
- Place your tomatoes over the cheese then evenly divide your spinach and tofu between them.
- Shape the tortillas into burritos.
- Enjoy.

Amount per serving (4 total)

Timing Information:

Preparation	10 m
Cooking	20 m
Total Time	30 m

Nutritional Information:

Calories	374 kcal
Fat	15.3 g
Carbohydrates	48.7g
Protein	22.5 g
Cholesterol	26 mg
Sodium	2261 mg

* Percent Daily Values are based on a 2,000 calorie diet.

BUFFALO APPLES

Ingredients

- 1 tbsp Dijon mustard
- 1 onion roll, split
- 1/4 apple, thinly sliced
- 1 slice Buffalo sauce-flavored Monterey jack cheese

Directions

- Coat your bread with mustard evenly then add the cheese and apple pieces to each.
- Form a sandwich and flatten it.
- Enjoy.

Amount per serving (1 total)

Timing Information:

Preparation	
Cooking	5 m
Total Time	5 m

Nutritional Information:

Calories	289 kcal
Fat	11.1 g
Carbohydrates	33.1g
Protein	13 g
Cholesterol	25 mg
Sodium	777 mg

* Percent Daily Values are based on a 2,000 calorie diet.

BUFFALO WINGS II

(ASIAN STYLE)

Ingredients

- 15 chicken wings
- 1/2 C. all-purpose flour
- oil for deep frying
- 1/4 C. butter
- 1/4 C. hot pepper sauce
- 1 tbsp chili-garlic sauce
- 1/2 tsp Thai red chili paste
- 2 tbsps Asian sweet chili sauce
- 2 tbsps honey

Directions

- Get a bowl, combine: chicken wings and flour.

- Get the wings covered in the flour evenly then place some plastic on the bowl and put everything in the fridge for 1.5 hrs.
- Get your oil hot for frying.
- At the same time with a low level of heat, begin to stir and heat the following for 7 mins: honey, butter, sweet chili sauce, hot sauce, chili paste, regular chili sauce.
- Cook your chicken in the oil for 13 mins until they are fully done then place the wings in a clean bowl.
- Add the sauce to the bowl and toss everything to evenly coat the wings.
- Enjoy.

Amount per serving (15 total)

Timing Information:

Preparation	10 m
Cooking	10 m
Total Time	1 h 20 m

Nutritional Information:

Calories	181 kcal
Fat	14.1 g
Carbohydrates	7.2g
Protein	6.5 g
Cholesterol	27 mg
Sodium	205 mg

* Percent Daily Values are based on a 2,000 calorie diet.

Buffalo Soup

Ingredients

- 2 bunches green onions, chopped
- 3 stalks celery, chopped
- 1/4 C. butter
- 1/4 C. flour
- 3/4 C. milk
- 3/4 C. chicken broth
- 2 C. diced cooked chicken
- 1/4-1/2 C. buffalo sauce
- 4 oz. process cheese
- 1/2 tsp cayenne
- 1/2 tsp celery salt
- 1/2 tsp garlic salt

Directions

- Stir fry your celery and onions in butter. Once everything is soft add in the flour and stir the mix.
- Now gradually add in your broth and milk.
- Stir the mix until it is smooth again then add in the: green onions, chicken, chicken sauce, cheese, cayenne, celery salt, and garlic salt.
- Stir the mix again and get everything hot.
- Continue cooking the mix until you find that the cheese is well combined then shut the heat.
- Enjoy.

Amount per serving: 4

Timing Information:

Preparation	25 mins
Total Time	55 mins

Nutritional Information:

Calories	394.5
Cholesterol	111.8mg
Sodium	769.9mg
Carbohydrates	16.7g
Protein	26.8g

* Percent Daily Values are based on a 2,000 calorie diet.

Buffalo Russets

Ingredients

- 1/3 C. melted butter
- 1 tsp cider vinegar
- 3 tsps hot sauce
- 1/2 tsp salt
- 4 russet potatoes, unpeeled, cut into wedges

Directions

- Get an outdoor grill hot.
- Get a bowl, combine: salt, butter, hot sauce, and vinegar.
- Stir the mix until the salt has dissolved then place the potatoes in the mix.
- Stir everything again to evenly coat the potatoes then place the potatoes on the grill.

- Place a lid on the grill and cook the potatoes for 30 mins while coating them with the hot sauce mix.
- Enjoy.

Amount per serving: 4

Timing Information:

Preparation	10 mins
Total Time	35 mins

Nutritional Information:

Calories	300.1
Cholesterol	40.6mg
Sodium	531.6mg
Carbohydrates	37.3g
Protein	4.4g

* Percent Daily Values are based on a 2,000 calorie diet.

BUFFALO VEGETARIAN WRAPS

Ingredients

- 1 whole wheat sandwich wrap
- 1/2 C. tomatoes, slices
- 1 C. chopped lettuce
- 1/2 C. extra firm tofu
- 2 tbsps ranch dressing
- 1/4 C. shredded cheddar cheese
- 2 tbsps buffalo, sauce
- 2 tbsps hot sauce

Directions

- Cube your tofu then stir fry them until browned all over.
- Pour in the buffalo and hot sauce and stir everything for 2 mins.
- Now lay your wraps and coat each one with the ranch.

- Lay your tomato and lettuce over the sauce then top everything with the tofu.
- Top the tofu with the cheese and some more hot sauce.
- Shape the wrap into a burrito.
- Enjoy.

Amount per serving: 1

Timing Information:

Preparation	5 mins
Total Time	15 mins

Nutritional Information:

Calories	368.8
Cholesterol	39.5mg
Sodium	533.3mg
Carbohydrates	9.0g
Protein	18.9g

* Percent Daily Values are based on a 2,000 calorie diet.

Buffalo Pretzels

Ingredients

- 1 tsp ground cayenne pepper
- 1 tsp lemon pepper
- 1 1/2 tsps garlic salt
- 1 (1 oz.) Ranch-style dressing mix
- 3/4 C. vegetable oil
- 1 1/2 (15 oz.) packages mini pretzels

Directions

- Get a bowl, combine: veggie oil, cayenne, ranch, lemon pepper, and garlic salt.
- Stir the mix until it is smooth then add in pretzels and stir everything again.
- Place a covering of plastic on the bowl and let the pretzels sit for 3 hrs in the mix then stir everything again.

- Enjoy.

Amount per serving (10 total)

Timing Information:

Preparation	
Cooking	5 m
Total Time	2 h 5 m

Nutritional Information:

Calories	161 kcal
Fat	16.5 g
Carbohydrates	3.4g
Protein	0.3 g
Cholesterol	< 0 mg
Sodium	553 mg

* Percent Daily Values are based on a 2,000 calorie diet.

SPICY MEATBALLS

Ingredients

- 2 lbs ground beef
- 1 egg
- 1/4 C. bread crumbs
- 1/2 C. uncooked white rice
- 2 tsps ground cumin
- 1/2 tsp garlic powder
- 1/4 tsp salt
- 10 C. chicken broth
- 4 carrots, sliced
- 1/2 large onion, chopped
- 4 stalks celery, sliced
- 1 (10 oz.) can diced tomatoes with green chili peppers
- 1 (8 oz.) can tomato sauce
- 1 (7 oz.) can diced green chilies, drained
- 1 bunch cilantro leaves, chopped

- 1/2 tsp garlic powder
- 1 tsp dried oregano
- 2 tsps ground cumin

Directions

- Get a bowl, combine: salt, beef, garlic powder, egg, cumin, rice, and bread crumbs.
- Stir the mix then get your broth boiling.
- Once the broth is boiling work the beef mix into balls then place them in the broth.
- Reduce the heat and cook the beef for 25 mins.
- Add in the cumin, carrots, oregano, onion, garlic powder, celery, cilantro, tomatoes with chilies, canned chilies, and tomato sauce.
- Stir the mix and continue cook everything for 65 more mins.
- Enjoy.

Amount per serving (10 total)

Timing Information:

Preparation	30 m
Cooking	1 h 20 m
Total Time	1 h 50 m

Nutritional Information:

Calories	289 kcal
Fat	13.4 g
Carbohydrates	17.9g
Protein	23.2 g
Cholesterol	75 mg
Sodium	1394 mg

* Percent Daily Values are based on a 2,000 calorie diet.

Buffalo Croutons

Ingredients

- 10 slices bread
- 5 tbsps ground dried chili pepper
- 5 tbsps garlic and herb seasoning
- 1 tbsp vegetable oil, or as needed

Directions

- Grab a C. and use it remove holes from your pieces of bread.
- Throw away the other portion of the bread or find a productive use for it (for example feeding birds in your backyard).
- Now top your bread circles with 3/4 tsp of the garlic spice and 3/4 tsp of chili.
- Fry the bread in oil for 4 mins each side.

- Then cut the circles into cubes or use the croutons as circles.
- Enjoy.

Amount per serving (5 total)

Timing Information:

Preparation	10 m
Cooking	10 m
Total Time	20 m

Nutritional Information:

Calories	157 kcal
Fat	4.4 g
Carbohydrates	25.3g
Protein	3.8 g
Cholesterol	0 mg
Sodium	340 mg

* Percent Daily Values are based on a 2,000 calorie diet.

Buffalo Scones

Ingredients

- 1 C. all-purpose flour
- 1 C. whole wheat flour
- 1/4 C. white sugar
- 4 tsps baking powder
- 1 1/2 tsps ground cinnamon
- 1/2 tsp ground nutmeg
- 1/2 tsp salt
- 1/4 tsp chili powder
- 1/3 C. margarine, chilled
- 1/2 C. currants
- 1 egg
- 2/3 C. milk
- 2 tbsps milk
- 2 tbsps white sugar

Directions

- Coat a cookie sheet with oil then set your oven to 425 degrees before doing anything else.
- Get a bowl, combine: salt, flour, chili powder, nutmeg, wheat flour, cinnamon, sugar, and baking powder.
- Stir the mix slowly then add the butter in pieces and keep mixing everything until the mix is crumbly then add in the raisins and mix everything again.
- Get a 2nd bowl for your eggs and whisk them. Combine the eggs with the flour mix and form a dough.
- Knead the dough for 5 mins then form the dough into 12 pieces.
- Flatten each piece and coat everything with sugar and milk.
- Cut an incision into each and place everything in the oven for 20 mins.
- Top the scones with some butter when eating them.
- Enjoy.

Amount per serving (12 total)

Timing Information:

Preparation	15 m
Cooking	15 m
Total Time	30 m

Nutritional Information:

Calories	174 kcal
Fat	6.1 g
Carbohydrates	27.5g
Protein	3.8 g
Cholesterol	17 mg
Sodium	331 mg

* Percent Daily Values are based on a 2,000 calorie diet.

Buffalo Burgers

Ingredients

- 2 lbs ground beef
- 2 tsps diced garlic
- 2 fresh jalapeno peppers, seeded and diced
- 1 small fresh poblano chili pepper, seeded and diced
- 1 fresh habanero pepper, seeded and diced
- 1 tsp crushed red pepper flakes
- 2 tbsps chopped fresh cilantro
- 1 tsp ground cumin

Directions

- Get a bowl, combine: cumin, beef, cilantro, garlic, pepper flakes, jalapenos, habanero, and poblano.
- Shape the meat into balls. Then flatten each ball.
- Get an outdoor grill hot then coat the grate with oil.

- Grill your burgers for 6 mins each side.
- Enjoy.

Amount per serving (8 total)

Timing Information:

Preparation	15 m
Cooking	10 m
Total Time	25 m

Nutritional Information:

Calories	232 kcal
Fat	16.4 g
Carbohydrates	1.1g
Protein	< 19.1 g
Cholesterol	70 mg
Sodium	67 mg

* Percent Daily Values are based on a 2,000 calorie diet.

BUFFALO KEBABS

Ingredients

- 4 lbs ground beef
- 1 lb spicy pork sausage
- 2 1/2 tsps mustard seed
- 2 1/2 tsps liquid smoke flavoring
- 1 tbsp Worcestershire sauce
- 1 tbsp garlic powder
- 5 tbsps sugar-based curing mixture
- 1 tbsp cracked black pepper
- 1 tbsp caraway seed
- 2 tsps cayenne pepper
- 2 tsps paprika
- 2 tsps chili powder
- 2 tsps red pepper flakes

Directions

- Get a bowl, combine: pepper flakes, beef, chili powder, paprika, cayenne, pork, caraway, mustard seed, black pepper, liquid smoke, curing salt, garlic powder, and Worcestershire.
- Place a covering of plastic on the bowl and put everything in the fridge for 8 hrs.
- Shape the meat into 6 cylinders then cover each with foil.
- Perforate the foil with a fork. Then set your oven to 200 degrees before doing anything else.
- Place the beef in a jelly roll pan and cook them in the oven for 6 hrs.
- Then shut the oven and let the meat sit for 4 more mins.
- Slice the cylinders into coins.
- Enjoy.

Amount per serving (15 total)

Timing Information:

Preparation	15 m
Cooking	6 h
Total Time	6 h 15 m

Nutritional Information:

Calories	310 kcal
Fat	21.9 g
Carbohydrates	2.3g
Protein	< 24.9 g
Cholesterol	91 mg
Sodium	2681 mg

* Percent Daily Values are based on a 2,000 calorie diet.

BUFFALO EGGPLANT

Ingredients

- 2 tbsps vegetable oil
- 4 eggplants, cut into 1-inch cubes
- 2 tbsps vegetable oil
- 2 onions, thinly sliced
- 1 tbsp diced garlic
- 2 tbsps soy sauce
- 2 tbsps water
- 1 1/2 tbsps oyster sauce
- 1 tbsp chili garlic sauce
- 1 tsp white sugar
- ground black pepper to taste
- 1/2 tsp Asian sesame oil

Directions

- Get a bowl, combine: black pepper, soy sauce, sugar, water, chili sauce, and oyster sauce. Stir the mix until it is smooth then place it to the side.
- Stir fry your eggplant in 2 tbsps of oil for 6 mins then place the veggies to the side.
- Add in another 2 tbsps of oil and begin to stir fry your onion for 1 min then add in the garlic and cook it for 1 more mins.
- Place the eggplant into the onion mix, set the heat to low, then add in the oyster sauce mix.
- Let everything gently boil for 7 mins then add some sesame oil and stir everything again.
- Enjoy.

Amount per serving (6 total)

Timing Information:

Preparation	20 m
Cooking	15 m
Total Time	35 m

Nutritional Information:

Calories	212 kcal
Fat	10.3 g
Carbohydrates	29.9g
Protein	5 g
Cholesterol	0 mg
Sodium	445 mg

* Percent Daily Values are based on a 2,000 calorie diet.

Buffalo Salsa

Ingredients

- 3 large ripe tomatoes, diced
- 3 roma (plum) tomatoes, diced
- 4 green onions, finely chopped
- 4 fresh jalapeno peppers, finely diced
- 1 stalk celery, finely diced
- 4 tbsps chopped fresh cilantro
- 1 clove garlic, diced
- 1 tbsp fresh lime juice
- 2 tsps ground black pepper
- salt to taste

Directions

- Get a bowl, combine: salt, tomatoes, pepper, plum tomatoes, lime juice, green onions, garlic, peppers, cilantro, and celery.
- Stir the mix to evenly coat the tomatoes then place a covering of plastic on the bowl and put everything in the fridge for 50 mins.
- Enjoy.

Amount per serving (20 total)

Timing Information:

Preparation	
Cooking	15 m
Total Time	1 h

Nutritional Information:

Calories	10 kcal
Fat	< 0.1 g
Carbohydrates	< 2.2g
Protein	< 0.5 g
Cholesterol	< 0 mg
Sodium	4 mg

* Percent Daily Values are based on a 2,000 calorie diet.

BUFFALO SOUP II

Ingredients

- 1 tsp unsalted butter
- 1/4 C. chopped celery
- 2 cloves garlic, chopped
- 1 tbsp all-purpose flour
- 3 1/2 C. chicken broth
- 1 1/2 C. chopped broccoli
- 1 1/2 C. cauliflower, chopped
- 2 tbsps peanut butter
- 1/4 tsp salt
- 1/4 tsp crushed red pepper flakes
- 2 green onions, chopped
- 1/4 C. heavy cream

Directions

- Stir fry your garlic and celery in butter for 7 mins then add in the flour and stir everything again.
- Let the mix fry for 60 secs then add in the pepper flakes, broth, salt, broccoli, peanut butter, and cauliflower.
- Let the mix gently boil for 17 mins then add in the green onions and cream and stir everything again.
- Enjoy.

Amount per serving (4 total)

Timing Information:

Preparation	15 m
Cooking	25 m
Total Time	40 m

Nutritional Information:

Calories	155 kcal
Fat	11.2 g
Carbohydrates	9.9g
Protein	5.4 g
Cholesterol	27 mg
Sodium	1058 mg

* Percent Daily Values are based on a 2,000 calorie diet.

BUFFALO FRUIT

Ingredients

- 1/4 tsp ground cumin
- 1/4 tsp ground coriander
- 1/4 tsp chili powder
- 1/4 tsp salt
- 1/8 tsp cayenne pepper
- 2 C. cubed seeded watermelon
- 1/2 lime, juiced

Directions

- Get a bowl, combine: cayenne, cumin, salt, coriander, and chili powder.
- Stir the mix slowly until it is smooth.
- Divide your fruit between serving platters and top the fruit with the spices.

- Top everything the lemon juice and let the plates sit for 5 mins then serve.
- Enjoy.

Amount per serving (2 total)

Timing Information:

Preparation	
Cooking	10 m
Total Time	10 m

Nutritional Information:

Calories	51 kcal
Fat	0.4 g
Carbohydrates	12.8g
Protein	1.1 g
Cholesterol	0 mg
Sodium	296 mg

* Percent Daily Values are based on a 2,000 calorie diet.

Buffalo Coconut Fish

Ingredients

- 1 C. unsweetened coconut milk
- 1/2 C. chopped fresh ginger root
- 1/2 C. chopped red onion
- 1 tsp chili powder
- salt to taste
- 1 mango, peeled, seeded and cubed
- 1 lb fresh swordfish, cut into chunks

Directions

- Get the following hot while stirring: salt, coconut milk, chili powder, ginger, and red onions.
- Stir the mix until the salt has dissolved then add in the mango and get everything boiling.

- Once the mix is boiling layer in your fish and set the heat to low.
- Let everything cook for 27 mins.
- Enjoy.

Amount per serving (4 total)

Timing Information:

Preparation	20 m
Cooking	30 m
Total Time	50 m

Nutritional Information:

Calories	302 kcal
Fat	17 g
Carbohydrates	14.7g
Protein	24.4 g
Cholesterol	44 mg
Sodium	120 mg

* Percent Daily Values are based on a 2,000 calorie diet.

BUFFALO SPINACH

Ingredients

- 5 oz. Pepper Jack cheese, shredded
- 1 (10 oz.) package frozen chopped spinach, thawed and drained
- 1/4 C. milk
- 1 tbsp sriracha

Directions

- Set your oven to 350 degrees before doing anything else.
- Get a casserole dish and add in: milk, spinach, and cheese.
- Stir the mix until it is smooth then cook it in the oven for 17 mins.
- Stir the mix twice as it cooks then add in your sriracha.
- Enjoy.

Amount per serving (8 total)

Timing Information:

Preparation	5 m
Cooking	20 m
Total Time	25 m

Nutritional Information:

Calories	84 kcal
Fat	6.1 g
Carbohydrates	2.5g
Protein	< 5.3 g
Cholesterol	20 mg
Sodium	137 mg

* Percent Daily Values are based on a 2,000 calorie diet.

Sriracha Chicken

Ingredients

- 4 skinless, boneless chicken breast halves
- 1 C. French salad dressing
- 1/4 C. salsa
- 1 tsp dried thyme
- 2 tbsps sriracha

Directions

- Coat a casserole dish with nonstick spray then set your oven to 350 degrees before doing anything else.
- Place your pieces of chicken in the dish then get a bowl and combine: thyme, dressing, and salsa.
- Top your meat with the dressing mix then place covering of foil over the dish.

- Cook everything in the oven for 25 mins then take off the covering and continue to cook the meat for 20 more mins.
- When 10 mins is left coat the chicken with the sriracha and continue cooking everything for 10 more mins.
- Enjoy.

Amount per serving (4 total)

Timing Information:

Preparation	10 m
Cooking	35 m
Total Time	45 m

Nutritional Information:

Calories	421 kcal
Fat	30.8 g
Carbohydrates	11g
Protein	25.3 g
Cholesterol	67 mg
Sodium	677 mg

* Percent Daily Values are based on a 2,000 calorie diet.

Buffalo Rotini

Ingredients

- 1 (12 oz.) package rotini pasta
- 1 tbsp vegetable oil
- 1 clove garlic, crushed
- 1 tsp dried basil
- 1 tsp Italian seasoning
- 1 onion, diced
- 2 red chili peppers, seeded and chopped
- 1 (14.5 oz.) can diced tomatoes
- 3 drops hot pepper sauce
- salt and ground black pepper to taste

Directions

- Get your pasta boiling in water and salt for 9 mins then remove all the liquids.

- At the same time begin to stir fry your Italian spice, basil, and garlic in oil for 5 mins then add in the chilies and onions.
- Continue frying everything until the onions are soft.
- Now combine in the hot sauce and the tomatoes as well.
- Keep cooking everything for 7 more mins then add the pasta some pepper and salt and stir the mix.
- Enjoy.

Amount per serving (6 total)

Timing Information:

Preparation	10 m
Cooking	20 m
Total Time	30 m

Nutritional Information:

Calories	134 kcal
Fat	2.8 g
Carbohydrates	22.5g
Protein	4.4 g
Cholesterol	0 mg
Sodium	117 mg

* Percent Daily Values are based on a 2,000 calorie diet.

BUFFALO RICE

Ingredients

- 2 tbsps margarine
- 1 large onion, chopped
- 1 large green bell pepper, chopped
- 1 red bell pepper, chopped
- 2 habanero peppers, chopped
- 3 lbs sirloin tips, thinly sliced
- 3 boneless skinless chicken breasts, cut into bite-size pieces
- 1 tbsp seasoned salt
- 3 tbsps vegetable oil, divided
- 4 C. uncooked long grain rice
- 4 cubes chicken bouillon
- 8 C. water
- 1 tsp garlic powder
- salt and ground black pepper to taste

Directions

- Stir fry the following in margarine: habanero, onion, red pepper, and green pepper.
- Continue to fry everything until the onions are see-through then place everything to the side.
- Coat your meats with the seasoned salt and begin to sear the meats in 1 tbsps of oil then place the meats to the side as well.
- Now toast your rice kernels in 2 tbsps of oil for 3 mins then add in the water and bouillon.
- Stir the rice until the bouillon is fully incorporated then add in the pepper, salt, garlic powder, meat, and peppers.
- Stir everything again, place a lid on the pan, and let the mix cook with a gentle boil for 22 mins, until the meats are fully done and the rice is done as well.
- Enjoy.

Amount per serving (10 total)

Timing Information:

Preparation	30 m
Cooking	25 m
Total Time	55 m

Nutritional Information:

Calories	719 kcal
Fat	28.4 g
Carbohydrates	63.1g
Protein	48.5 g
Cholesterol	132 mg
Sodium	891 mg

* Percent Daily Values are based on a 2,000 calorie diet.

CAYENNE PRAWNS

Ingredients

- 1 large clove garlic
- 1 tbsp coarse salt
- 1/2 tsp cayenne pepper
- 1 tsp paprika
- 2 tbsps olive oil
- 2 tsps lemon juice
- 2 lbs large shrimp, peeled and deveined
- 8 wedges lemon, for garnish

Directions

- Get a bowl, combine: salt and garlic.
- Mash everything together then add in the lemon juice, cayenne, olive oil, and paprika.

- Stir the mix until it is smooth then add in your shrimp and stir everything again.
- Get your grill hot then coat the grate with oil.
- Grill your shrimp for 4 mins then flip them and continue grilling the pieces for 4 more mins.
- Serve the dish with the lemon.
- Enjoy.

Amount per serving (6 total)

Timing Information:

Preparation	15 m
Cooking	6 m
Total Time	21 m

Nutritional Information:

Calories	164 kcal
Fat	5.9 g
Carbohydrates	2.7g
Protein	< 25.1 g
Cholesterol	230 mg
Sodium	1226 mg

* Percent Daily Values are based on a 2,000 calorie diet.

BUFFALO BEANS

Ingredients

- 3/4 lb fresh green beans, trimmed
- 2 tbsps soy sauce
- 1 clove garlic, diced
- 1 tsp garlic chili sauce
- 1 tsp honey
- 2 tsps canola oil

Directions

- Steam your green beans with a steamer insert over 2 inches of boiling water, with a lid placed on a large pot.
- Cook the veggies for 5 mins then get a bowl and combine: the honey, soy sauce, chili sauce, and garlic.
- Begin to stir fry the beans for 4 mins then add in the sauce and continue frying everything for 3 more mins.

- Enjoy.

Amount per serving (4 total)

Timing Information:

Preparation	15 m
Cooking	10 m
Total Time	25 m

Nutritional Information:

Calories	59 kcal
Fat	2.4 g
Carbohydrates	8.6g
Protein	2.1 g
Cholesterol	0 mg
Sodium	513 mg

* Percent Daily Values are based on a 2,000 calorie diet.

Buffalo Beef

Ingredients

- 1/4 C. cornstarch
- 1/4 tbsp salt
- black pepper
- 12 oz. flank steak, thinly sliced
- 1 quart oil for frying
- 4 tbsps soy sauce
- 1 tbsp rice vinegar
- 1/2 tbsp rice wine
- 1 1/2 tbsps honey
- 7 tbsps granulated sugar
- 1/2 tbsp chili paste
- 1/4 C. water
- 3 tbsps chopped fresh ginger root
- 1 tbsp vegetable oil
- 2 cloves garlic, chopped

- 1/4 C. sliced onion
- 1/4 C. diced red bell pepper

Directions

- Get your oil hot.
- Get a bowl, combine: pepper, cornstarch, and salt.
- Dredge your steak in the mix then fry the meat in the oil until it is browned all over.
- Now get a 2nd bowl, combine: honey, soy sauce, rice wine, and rice vinegar.
- Stir the mix until it is smooth then add in the ginger, sugar, water, and chili paste.
- Stir the mix again.
- Now get a wok and begin to stir fry your pepper, garlic, and onions for 1 mins then add in the sauce and cook everything for 1 more min.
- Now combine in the meat and get everything hot and evenly coated.
- Enjoy.

Amount per serving (4 total)

Timing Information:

Preparation	20 m
Cooking	20 m
Total Time	45 m

Nutritional Information:

Calories	489 kcal
Fat	31.8 g
Carbohydrates	40.9g
Protein	11.4 g
Cholesterol	27 mg
Sodium	1383 mg

* Percent Daily Values are based on a 2,000 calorie diet.

CHILI BAKED POTATOES

Ingredients

- 5 medium red potatoes, diced with peel
- 1 medium onion, chopped
- 1 tbsp garlic powder
- 1 tbsp kosher salt
- 2 tsps chili powder
- 1/4 C. extra virgin olive oil
- 1 C. shredded Cheddar cheese

Directions

- Set your oven to 450 degrees before doing anything else.
- Place your potatoes in a casserole dish that has been coated with nonstick spray then add in your onions as well.

- Top everything with the chili powder, garlic powder, and salt.
- Stir the mix. Then cook everything in the oven for 45 mins.
- Stir the mix every 15 mins then top the potatoes with cheese and let it melt.
- Enjoy.

Amount per serving (4 total)

Timing Information:

Preparation	15 m
Cooking	40 m
Total Time	55 m

Nutritional Information:

Calories	473 kcal
Fat	26.1 g
Carbohydrates	47.6g
Protein	14.4 g
Cholesterol	36 mg
Sodium	1685 mg

* Percent Daily Values are based on a 2,000 calorie diet.

Easy Buffalo Wings III

Ingredients

- 6 lbs chicken wings, separated at joints, tips discarded
- 1 1/2 C. Louisiana-style hot sauce
- 3/4 C. butter
- 1 C. honey
- 1 pinch garlic salt
- 1 pinch ground black pepper
- 1 tsp cayenne pepper, or to taste

Directions

- Grill your chicken for 10 mins per side. Then place the meat in a baking dish.
- Begin to heat and stir the following in a pot: cayenne, hot sauce, black pepper, butter, garlic salt, and honey.

- Let the mix gently boil for 12 mins then top the chicken with the sauce and stir everything to evenly cover the wings with sauce.
- Enjoy.

Amount per serving (12 total)

Timing Information:

Preparation	15 m
Cooking	30 m
Total Time	45 m

Nutritional Information:

Calories	356 kcal
Fat	22.7 g
Carbohydrates	23.9g
Protein	15.6 g
Cholesterol	78 mg
Sodium	896 mg

* Percent Daily Values are based on a 2,000 calorie diet.

Buffalo Pickles

Ingredients

- 12 3 to 4 inch long pickling cucumbers
- 2 C. water
- 1 3/4 C. white vinegar
- 1 1/2 C. chopped fresh dill weed
- 1/2 C. white sugar
- 8 cloves garlic, chopped
- 1 1/2 tbsps coarse salt
- 1 tbsp pickling spice
- 1 1/2 tsps dill seed
- 1/2 tsp red pepper flakes, or to taste
- 4 sprigs fresh dill weed

Directions

- Get a bowl, combine: pepper flakes, cucumbers, dill seed, water, pickling spice, vinegar, salt, chopped dill, garlic, and sugar.
- Combine the mix until it is smooth and leave it for 3 hrs.
- Get 3 Mason jar and place 4 cucumbers in each.
- Divide your mix between the jars and place the lids on tightly after adding some fresh dill to each one.
- Place the pickles in the fridge for 12 days.
- Enjoy.

Amount per serving (12 total)

Timing Information:

Preparation	
Cooking	15 m
Total Time	10 d 2 h 15 m

Nutritional Information:

Calories	70 kcal
Fat	0.3 g
Carbohydrates	< 16.9g
Protein	1.6 g
Cholesterol	0 mg
Sodium	728 mg

* Percent Daily Values are based on a 2,000 calorie diet.

BUFFALO TACOS

Ingredients

- 1 yam, peeled and diced
- 1 tbsp olive oil
- 3/4 lb ground turkey
- 1/2 C. chopped sweet onion
- 1 clove garlic, diced
- 4 jalapeno peppers, seeded and diced
- 1 tbsp chili powder
- 1 tsp ground cumin
- 1/2 tsp Cajun seasoning
- 1/2 tsp salt
- 1/2 C. tomatillo salsa
- 1/2 C. chopped fresh cilantro
- 16 warm flour tortillas

Directions

- Cook your yams in the microwave for 8 mins.
- Now coat a frying pan with olive oil and stir fry the turkey for 8 mins.
- Add in the jalapenos, garlic, and onions to the pan and continue to fry everything for 8 more mins.
- Now add in the salt, chili powder, Cajun spice, and cumin.
- Top the turkey with the salsa then stir everything.
- Add in the yams and stir the mix again.
- Let everything cool off a bit then evenly divide the mix between your tortillas after warming them.
- Now coat your tacos with some cilantro.
- Enjoy.

Amount per serving (8 total)

Timing Information:

Preparation	20 m
Cooking	25 m
Total Time	45 m

Nutritional Information:

Calories	602 kcal
Fat	16.4 g
Carbohydrates	91.1g
Protein	21.6 g
Cholesterol	31 mg
Sodium	1182 mg

* Percent Daily Values are based on a 2,000 calorie diet.

Buffalo Salmon

Ingredients

- 1 1/2 tsps ground black pepper
- 1/2 tsp paprika
- 1/4 tsp cayenne pepper
- 1 tsp diced garlic
- 1 tbsp Dijon mustard
- 1 tbsp brown sugar
- 1/2 tsp onion powder
- 1/4 tsp salt
- 1 tbsp olive oil
- 2 (6 oz.) salmon fillets
- 2 tbsps olive oil
- 1 1/2 tbsps diced onion
- 1 tbsps sriracha

Directions

- Get a bowl, combine: salt, black pepper, onion powder, paprika, brown sugar, cayenne, Dijon, and diced garlic.
- Stir the mix until it is evenly combined. Then add in 1 tbsp of olive oil and stir everything again.
- Coat your pieces of fish with the mix then place the fish in a casserole dish and let them sit for 40 mins with a covering of plastic on the dish.
- Begin to stir fry your onions for 12 mins in 2 tbsps of olive oil then add in the fish and fry them for 5 mins each side.
- When serving the fish top them with the onions and also the oil from the pan and the sriracha.
- Enjoy.

Amount per serving (2 total)

Timing Information:

Preparation	10 m
Cooking	10 m
Total Time	50 m

Nutritional Information:

Calories	496 kcal
Fat	36.6 g
Carbohydrates	11.3g
Protein	29.5 g
Cholesterol	83 mg
Sodium	562 mg

* Percent Daily Values are based on a 2,000 calorie diet.

Cajun Pasta

Ingredients

- 1/2 C. vegetable oil
- 8 oz. tomato sauce
- 1 C. water
- 1/4 tsp dried basil
- 1 tsp ground black pepper
- 1 tsp crushed red pepper flakes
- 1 tsp salt
- 1 lb small shrimp, peeled and deveined
- 1 green bell pepper, chopped
- 1 red bell pepper, chopped
- 1/2 onion, chopped
- 3 cloves garlic, diced
- 2 tsps cornstarch
- 1 fluid oz. cold water
- 12 oz. spaghetti

- 8 green onions, diced

Directions

- In a pot combine the following: 1/2 tsp salt, 4 oz. oil, 1/2 tsp pepper flakes, tomato sauce, 1/2 tsp black pepper, 10 oz. of water, and basil.
- Stir the mix and get everything boiling.
- Once the mix is boiling set the heat to low.
- Get a bowl, combine: 1/2 tsp pepper flakes, 1/2 tsp salt, 1/2 tsp black pepper, and the shrimp.
- Evenly coat the shrimp with the spices then place everything to the side.
- In a separate pot begin to stir fry your bell peppers, garlic, and onions in 1 oz. of oil for 7 mins then add these veggies to the tomato sauce.
- Let the veggies cook for 5 mins with a medium level of heat then set the heat to low again and cook everything for 30 mins.
- Stir the mix every 10 mins.

- After 20 mins of simmering the tomato sauce and veggies add in the shrimp and continue simmering the mix for 10 more mins with a medium level of heat to fully cook the shrimp.
- Get a bowl, combine: 1 oz. water and cornstarch.
- Stir the mix until it is smooth then combine it with the simmering tomato sauce mix when 5 mins of time is left.
- Now get your pasta boiling in water and salt for 9 mins, in a separate pot then remove all the liquids.
- Divide your pasta into bowls for serving.
- Then liberally top each serving with tomato sauce and some green onions.
- Enjoy.

Amount per serving (5 total)

Timing Information:

Preparation	10 m
Cooking	1 h 30 m
Total Time	1 h 40 m

Nutritional Information:

Calories	585 kcal
Fat	25 g
Carbohydrates	61g
Protein	29 g
Cholesterol	138 mg
Sodium	845 mg

* Percent Daily Values are based on a 2,000 calorie diet.

CREOLE CAKE

Ingredients

- 3 C. all-purpose flour
- 1 1/2 C. white sugar
- 2 tsps baking soda
- 1/4 tsp salt
- 2 eggs
- 1 (20 oz.) can crushed pineapple with juice

Topping:

- 3/4 C. white sugar
- 3/4 C. evaporated milk
- 1/2 C. margarine
- 1 C. chopped pecans
- 1 1/2 C. flaked coconut

Directions

- Coat a casserole dish with flour and oil then set your oven to 350 degrees before doing anything else.
- Get a bowl combine: baking soda, flour, salt, and 1.5 C. of sugar.
- Stir the mix then combine in the pineapple with liquid, and the eggs. Get an electric mixer and combine everything for 1 min with a low speed.
- Enter everything into the casserole dish then cook it all in the oven for 32 mins.
- At the same time get the following boiling: margarine, milk, and 3/4 C. of sugar.
- Let the mix cook for 3 mins while whisking everything together then add in the coconut and the pecans.
- Now shut the heat and top the cake with the coconut mix.
- Enjoy.

Amount per serving (12 total)

Timing Information:

Preparation	30 m
Cooking	1 h
Total Time	1 h 30 m

Nutritional Information:

Calories	492 kcal
Fat	19 g
Carbohydrates	76.5g
Protein	6.8 g
Cholesterol	36 mg
Sodium	402 mg

* Percent Daily Values are based on a 2,000 calorie diet.

THANKS FOR READING! NOW LET'S TRY SOME **SUSHI** AND **DUMP DINNERS**....

http://bit.ly/2443TFg

To grab this **box set** simply follow the link mentioned above, or tap the book cover.

This will take you to a page where you can simply enter your email address and a PDF version of the **box set** will be emailed to you.

I hope you are ready for some serious cooking!

http://bit.ly/2443TFg

You will also receive updates about all my new books when they are free.

Also don't forget to like and subscribe on the social networks. I love meeting my readers. Links to all my profiles are below so please click and connect :)

Facebook

Twitter

COME ON...
LET'S BE FRIENDS :)

I adore my readers and love connecting with them socially. Please follow the links below so we can connect on Facebook, Twitter, and Google+.

Facebook

Twitter

I also have a blog that I regularly update for my readers so check it out below.

My Blog

CAN I ASK A FAVOUR?

If you found this book interesting, or have otherwise found any benefit in it. Then may I ask that you post a review of it on Amazon? Nothing excites me more than new reviews, especially reviews which suggest new topics for writing. I do read all reviews and I always factor feedback into my newer works.

So if you are willing to take ten minutes to write what you sincerely thought about this book then please visit our Amazon page and post your opinions.

Again thank you!

INTERESTED IN OTHER EASY COOKBOOKS?

Everything is easy! Check out my Amazon Author page for more great cookbooks:

For a complete listing of all my books please see my author page.

Made in the USA
Lexington, KY
14 October 2016